CW01188655

HEATH ROBINSON
BRITAIN AT PLAY

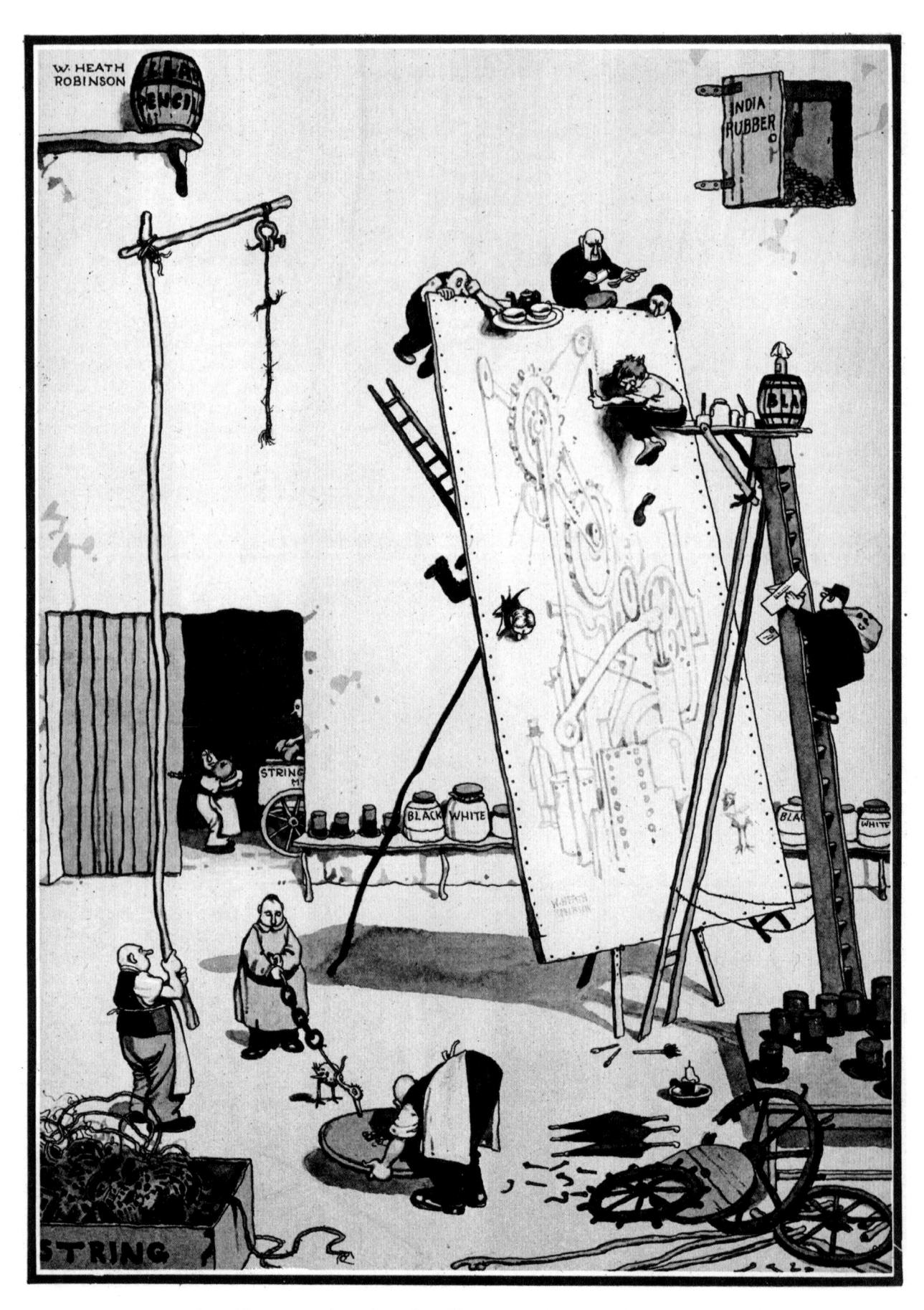

A Heath Robinson Drawing of Heath Robinson Drawing a Heath Robinson Drawing.
Drawing a piece of String from Life, showing the consummate accuracy of this artist, to attain
which he spares neither time, nor indeed his own personal safety.

HEATH ROBINSON
BRITAIN AT PLAY

Edited by Geoffrey Beare

DUCKWORTH

This edition published in 2023 by Duckworth,
an imprint of Duckworth Books Ltd,
1 Golden Court, Richmond, TW9 1EU, United Kingdom
www.duckworthbooks.co.uk

First published in 2008 by Duckworth Overlook

Copyright © 2008 The Estate of Mrs J.C. Robinson
Text copyright © 2008 by Geoffrey Beare

All rights reserved. No part of this publication
may be reproduced, stored in a retrieval system, or
transmitted, in any form or by any means, electronic,
mechanical, photocopying, recording or otherwise,
without the prior permission of the publisher.

A catalogue record for this book is available
from the British Library

ISBN 9780715655313

Printed and bound in the UK by
Bell and Bain Ltd, Glasgow

INTRODUCTION

At the end of his life William Heath Robinson was famous as 'The Gadget King' and it is for his drawings of contraptions, collected in the previous volume in this series, that he is still most widely known. However, these mechanical devices were the subject for only about a quarter of his humorous output. The remainder feature a wide range of subject matter, partly deriving from his own interests, but to a large extent driven by the requirements of the editors of the periodicals for which he worked.

He started his career working as a serious illustrator of books and periodicals, quickly establishing himself as one of the leading artists in his field. In 1904 a publisher for whom he was working declared himself bankrupt, leaving Heath Robinson unpaid for a large body of work. He had recently married and had a baby daughter, so needed rapidly to find a new source of income. He turned to the quality weekly magazines such as *The Tatler*, *The Sketch*, *The Illustrated Sporting and Dramatic News* and later *The Bystander* which featured a number of full-page humorous drawings in each issue and would pay for each drawing as it was delivered. *The Sketch* advertised itself as 'pre-eminent for its illustrations of the theatre, to say nothing of society, sport and art' and its competitors had a similar range of interests with the emphasis on sport. Their readers were predominantly the moneyed upper- and upper-middle classes and so it is their preoccupations that feature in the drawings. The range is extended by the work that he did for the middle-class monthly magazines such as *The Strand* and *Pearson's* and, later, the *Humorist*.

Many of Heath Robinson's drawings feature people at work, but in this volume I have collected a wide range of drawings relating to 'Britain at Play', whether in the home or outside it, including some examples of what Heath Robinson thought makes us British. By far the largest proportion of such drawings relates to various sports and games, and of those the dominant topic is golf. Heath Robinson was not himself a golfer (despite the drawing of himself on the first tee), which perhaps explains why he was so willing to emphasise the more ridiculous aspects of the game and those who play it. He captures their obsessive streak and their preoccupation with special clothing and gadgets. The potential absurdity of the game is captured in the series 'Aquatic Golf'. A collection of his golfing cartoons, *The Humours of Golf*, was published both in Britain and in the USA in 1923.

More seasonal sports for the readers of *The Bystander* were hunting, shooting, fishing and winter sports. Heath Robinson's earliest successful series of humorous drawings appeared in *The Sketch* under the title 'The Gentle Art of Catching Things'. Originally published in black and white, six of the subjects were reprinted in full colour by Valentine's as postcards. These show a degree of wild surrealism that was gradually tamed, although not completely suppressed, by art editors. Less grotesque, but as exuberant in its fantasy, is the drawing 'A remarkable incidence of quick skating' made some 13 years later. Equally surreal are the transpositions of three of Howard Elcock's sophisticated Monte Carlo socialites into the ski resort of Grindelwald populated by Heath Robinson's plump, bespectacled skiers and of a number of Robinson's winter sports enthusiasts into Elcock's Monte Carlo. Other featured sports include cricket and rugby (but hardly ever soccer), tennis and swimming. Another popular source of seasonal subject matter was the family holiday and the seaside.

As anyone who has read his autobiography will be aware, Heath Robinson was, at heart, a romantic. Scenes of courtship and respectable love-making always appealed to him. The possibilities of mistletoe provided opportunities to link such subjects to a seasonal theme, and to demonstrate the ingenuity of lovers in taking the chances for romance that it provided, as is delightfully demonstrated in 'Opportunity' or ''Tis an ill wind that . . .'. Even water-snails are not immune from the influence of the magic branch. Equally fascinating was the frustrated kiss, prevented by the falling of an autumn leaf, or not quite achieved in 'A Near Thing'.

It was Heath Robinson's increasing celebrity as a humorist that led him into the world of broadcasting. In April 1923 an unusual competition run by *The Bystander* introduced him to radio broadcasting. The competition was called 'Drawings by Wireless'. Heath Robinson, speaking from the studio at London's radio station 2LO, described to listeners a drawing he had made of the difficulties of erecting an aerial. Those wishing to participate in the competition were then invited to make a sketch in the style of Mr. Heath Robinson and to send it to *The Bystander*. The winning entry would be the one that came closest to the original drawing that had been described. A prize of ten guineas was offered and the best drawings were published in a subsequent issue of the magazine. The winning

Heath Robinson's drawing for the radio competition.

The winning entry.

entry looks more like the artist's published work than the simple sketch that he had prepared for the broadcast! Radio continued to provide subject matter for his drawings through the 1920s.

Heath Robinson was a distinctly British artist and it can be argued that a clear strain of Britishness runs through most of his work. One aspect of this is what he once called 'Mark Tapley-ism', referring to the character in Martin Chuzzlewit who put great store by remaining cheerful in adversity. This characteristic is beautifully illustrated in the series 'The Right Spirit'. Similarly, the British character is exemplified in the 1909 series of 'A Few Virtues' and in the Boy Scout ethos portrayed in the series of good turns illustrated in the 'Jamboree of Laughter'.

Motoring, gardening and home life all provided fertile ground for his magazine illustrations. Although never a motorist himself, he was always alert to the absurd possibilities of the subject, especially in the early days of the motor car. He was a keen gardener, although photographs of him in his garden show him using only the most conventional of implements. He was also a home-loving body, and when not in his studio would most likely be found sitting in his armchair with a cat curled up at his feet, reading and smoking his pipe. These topics provided the subject matter for the series of 'How to ...' books that he wrote first with KRG Brown and then with Cecil Hunt. The illustrated article 'A Complicated Science' published in *The Strand Magazine* in 1938 was the precursor to the third book in the series, *How to Make a Garden Grow*, published later the same year.

This collection of drawings looks at Heath Robinson's work from the viewpoint of 'Britain at Play', and has provided the opportunity to unearth a great deal of material not seen since it was first published in magazines.

Geoffrey Beare.

CONTENTS

GOLF 11
Aquatic Golf (*Strand*, 1922) **12-15**
Pogo golf – putting on the second green (*Bystander*, 1921) **16**
HR's new insurance scheme for golfers (*Bystander*, 1922) **17**
On the Fair Way (*Bystander*, 1923) **18**
Annual "Get-There-First" golfing competition (*Bystander*, 1923) **19**
We can quite believe it (WHR on first tee) (*Bystander*, 1923) **20**
An unfortunate back-hander at St. Andrews (*Bystander*, 1923) **21**
Down to bedrock (*Bystander*, 1923) **22**
A hefty Slice (*Bystander*, 1923) **23**
The kind caddy-bird of St. Andrews (*Bystander*, 1924) **24**
Casabianca of the links (*Bystander*, 1925) **25**
Another illustrated crossword puzzlette (*Bystander*, 1925) **26**
A Striking Example (*Bystander*, 1925) **27**
The Top Notcher (*Bystander*, 1925) **28**
"Here Comes the Bogey Man" (*Bystander*, 1926) **29**
The Lie (*Bystander*, 1926) **30**
Incurable (*Humorist*, 1931) **31**
Strange things that don't often happen at golf (*Humorist*, 1932) **32**

WINTER SPORTS 33
A remarkable instance of quick skating (*Bystander*, 1919) **34**
"It's an ill wind" (*Bystander*, 1922) **35**
A few trot-skis in Switzerland (*Bystander*, 1923) **36**
Safety Skating (*Royal*, 1924) **37**
A New Winter Sport ... the Luge Glider (*Royal*, 1924) **38**
A little pride before a fall (*Bystander*, 1924) **39**
Sorry, but this was bound to happen sometime! (*Bystander*, 1927) **40-41**
The new winter service (*Bystander*, 1925) **42**

HUNTING, SHOOTING AND FISHING 43
The Gentle Art of Catching Things (Valentine postcards, 1909) **44-49**
Landing an Anchovy on the Welsh Harp at Hendon (*Illustrated Sporting and Dramatic News*, 1912) **50**
"Grousing" in the Valley of the Thames (*Illustrated Sporting and Dramatic News*, 1912) **51**
Birdsnesting in the Adirondaks (nk, circa 1907) **52**
The man who didn't care (*Bystander*, 1919) **53**
A new exercise for fishing from an open boat (*Bystander*, 1922) **54**
A Moving Picture (*Bystander*, 1923) **55**
The bite. A striking example of how patience is rewarded (*Bystander*, 1925) **56**
The Vicious Circle (*Bystander*, 1925) **57**
How to catch a tiger (*BBC Yearbook*, 1930) **58**
Something on Each Way – A Fish Tragedy (*Humorist*, 1931) **59**
Tarpon Fishing de Luxe (*Passing Show*, 1931) **60**

OTHER SPORTS AND GAMES 61
A gentle game of rugby in the botanical gardens (*Illustrated Sporting and Dramatic News*, 1912) **62**
Cricket: Eton vs Harrow at Lords (*Illustrated Sporting and Dramatic News*, 1912) **63**

Gathering Edelweiss in the Pyrenees (*Printer's Pie*, 1910) **64**
When May is out – Casting Clouts (*Sketch*, 1915) **65**
Phizz-jerks (*Strand*, 1919) **66-69**
The Chukker Chucked (*Bystander*, 1919) **70**
Monte-Carlo reformed – filberts (*Bystander*, 1921) **71**
Lawn tennis for the middle aged (*Bystander*, 1921) **72**
Safety First – A cricket forecast for 1922 (*Bystander*, 1922) **73**
More Rugger Trials (*Bystander*, 1923) **74**
Silly points: how cricket is played in mountainous districts (*Bystander*, 1924) **75**
Clock Cricket (*Bystander*, 1925) **76**
Putting them on their metal (*Bystander*, 1925) **77**
The new craze of jazz tennis (*Bystander*, 1926) **78**
Another Wash-Out (*Bystander*, 1926) **79**
Some ingenious suggestions for giving the bowler a better chance (*Bystander*, 1927) **80**
Quick cricket (*Bystander*, 1927) **81**
Cue-ball – a new indoor game (*Sportsman (US)*, ca. 1930) **82**
Learning to Swim (*Humorist*, 1933) **83**
Men will be boys (*Christmas Pie*, 1936) **84**

ON HOLIDAY 85
The end of a perfect day (*Bystander*, 1919) **86**
The New Aerobathing Machine (*Bystander*, 1920) **87**
Curious optical illusion (*Bystander*, 1920) **88**
Some new water sports for the holidays (*Bystander*, 1921) **89**
More new water sports for the holidays (*Bystander*, 1921) **90**
But if you can't afford a real seaside holiday – why not try a dust-bath in Regent's Park (*Pearson's*, 1921) **91**
The start of the brighter seaside campaign (*Bystander*, 1924) **92**
My sweetie went away (*Bystander*, 1924) **93**
A Brine Wave (*Bystander*, 1924) **94**
The intellectual summer holiday (*Bystander*, 1925) **95**
Foot-sprints on the sands of time (*Bystander*, 1925) **96**
Getting fed up (*Bystander*, 1926) **97**
The cleaner bathing movement (*Bystander*, 1926) **98**
The transit of venus (*Bystander*, 1927) **99**
Doing his whack (*Bystander*, 1927) **100**
"Give" and take (*Bystander*, 1927) **101**
Sensible measures to be taken in the event of a heatwave (*Humorist*, 1929) **102**
Strenuous endeavours to keep the family cool on a warm day at Southend (*Sunday Graphic*, 1929) **103**
Remarkable presence of mind of cinematographer (*Passing Show*, 1929) **104**
Grateful Shade (*Humorist*, 1935) **105**
Humorist Cover July 1936 **106**
"Quick Lunch" – Cover for Whitsun Holiday special number (*Humorist*, 1939) **107**
The Disturbed Nap (*Humorist*, 1938) **108**
Free Seats (*Humorist*, 1938) **109**
New Seaside Sports (*Humorist*, 1939) **110**

MOTORING 111
Cartastrophies (*Out and Away*, 1919) **112-117**
Elasticity (*Passing Show*, nk) **118**
The Water Coupe (*Passing Show*, 1930) **119**
A heavy snowstorm — and a rapid thaw (*Humorist*, 1930) **120-121**
An Awkward Predicament (*Humorist*, 1930) **122**

CONTENTS

COURTING 123
The Reprimand (*Printer's Pie*, 1911) **124**
How the trains get delayed (*Bystander*, 1919) **125**
The "write" of way. Love at first sight (*Bystander*, 1923) **126**
The fall of the year (*Bystander*, 1924) **127**
Wherefore art thou radio? (*Bystander*, 1925) **128**
The maid and the magician. A real-life film in three terrible reels! (*Bystander*, 1925) **129**
"Oh, will thou be my Valentine" (*Bystander*, 1927) **130**
"'Tis an ill wind that ..." (*Strand*, 1929) **131**
Hoisting the Chaperone (*Humorist*, 1930) **132**
The Language of Eggs (*Humorist*, 1933) **133**
Opportunity (*Humorist*, 1936) **134**
A near thing (*Strand*, 1937) **135**
The sad story of a punctured romance (*Bystander*, 1926) **136**

AT HOME 137
Mother's help (*Sketch*, 1911) **138**
Breakfast (*Bystander*, 1920) **139**
The disorder of the bath (*Bystander*, 1920) **140**
Sleeping Arrangements (*Bystander*, 1920) **141**
Getting out of the house (*Bystander*, 1920) **142**
Coming down to breakfast (*Bystander*, 1920) **143**
His only shaving glass (*Bystander*, 1920) **144**
Leading from dummy (*Bystander*, 1924) **145**
Reforming the Dance (*Bystander*, 1920) **146**
Mrs Snifkin, dreamily, as she smells burning – "Dear! Dear! ..." (*Bystander*, 192?) **147**
Weighty Matters – An unrecorded eclipse of the sun (*Bystander*, 1927) **148**
Pets' corners, Boldersbury Mansions, SW (*How to live in a Flat*, 1936) **149**
The extending bungalow for weekend parties (*How to live in a Flat*, 1936) **150**

RADIO 151
My delicate aerial – modern style (*Bystander*, 1923) **152**
Listening in – that aerial vibration (*Bystander*, 1922) **153**
A wireless (up)set (*Bystander*, 1923) **154**
A stormy night at the listening inn (*Bystander*, 1923) **155**
The timely call of a new world (*Bystander*, 1924) **156**
Up the Bole (*Bystander*, 1926) **157**
A Bedtime Story (*Bystander*, 1927) **158**
The Broadcast Play (*Passing Show*, 1927) **159**
Some new wireless tests (*BBC Year Book*, 1930) **160**

THE BRITISH CHARACTER 161
A Few Virtues (*Pearson's*, 1909) **162-165**
A Jamboree of Laughter (*Fragments*, 1920) **166-171**
"An Englishman never knows when he is eaten" (*Bystander*, 1927) **172**
The Right Spirit (*Strand*, 1938) **173-180**

GARDENING 181
More Hints to Amateur Gardeners (*Pearson's*, 1923) **182-184**
The new fruit tree pruner (*Bystander*, ca. 1926) **185**
Hints for the Amateur Landscape Gardener (*Humorist*, 1931) **186**

A Highly Complicated Science (*Strand*, 1938) **187-191**

Acknowledgements **192**

GOLF

A Birdie.

Aquatic Golf

By W. HEATH ROBINSON

The Tee.

AQUATIC GOLF

A Common Mistake and Bunkered.

AQUATIC GOLF

The Lost Ball.

AQUATIC GOLF

Fore! and The Green.

GOLF

Pogo golf – putting on the second green.

GOLF

"Sign Now". Risks and liabilities covered by Heath Robinson's new insurance scheme for golfers.

GOLF

On the Fair Way. A touching story of the tired golfer and the kindly caddie.

Annual "Get-There-First" golfing competition – Takes Place as Usual at Tooting Bec.

We Can Quite Believe It. A portrait of the artist driving off the first tee.

GOLF

A Parting Shot. An unfortunate back-hander at St. Andrews.

21

GOLF

Down to bedrock. An intelligent method of overcoming a difficult problem.

A hefty Slice. The tragedy of the too-vigorous putt.

GOLF

Far Fetched. A lesson in unnatural history.
The kind caddie-bird of St. Andrews pursuing its daily round.

GOLF

Casabianca of the Links! –"Whence all but he had fled!".
A modern tragedy of our missing links, featuring a Boy of the Bulldog breed.

GOLF

A Very Cross Word Puzzle! "Across: A forceful exclamation!"

A Striking Example.
The sort of thing that convinces one of the necessity of lightening conductors on golf courses.

GOLF

A Top-Notcher! One of the silly mistakes one makes when it snows in Scotland.

GOLF

"Here Comes the Bogey Man".
How you can detect the good golfer from the ordinary man in the street.

The Lie. One of those golfing stories which you are bound
not to believe if you don't want to.

GOLF

The incurable golfer does a short hole in one.

Strange things that don't often happen at golf.

WINTER SPORTS

A remarkable instance of quick skating – a gentleman leaves his shadow behind.

WINTER SPORTS

"It's an ill wind ..." Native Swiss profiting by the misfortunes of an eminent skier.

35

Wild and Woolly. A few trot-skis in Switzerland.

Safety Skating.

WINTER SPORTS

A New Winter Sport ... the Luge Glider.

A little pride before a fall. Remarkable presence of mind of one ski-ist
called forth by the carelessness of a companion.

WINTER SPORTS

Sorry, but this was bound to happen sometime! ...

WINTER SPORTS

... Extraordinary happenings at Grindelcarlo and Montewald. (Mr Howard Elcock's sophisticated inhabitants of the Côte d'Azur stray into the world of Heath Robinson's winter sporting enthusiasts and vice versa.)

The new winter service. Devotees of Rug-tennis, the new game which enables Rugby players to avoid getting stale at half-time, demonstrating their skill.

HUNTING, SHOOTING AND FISHING

THE GENTLE ART OF CATCHING THINGS

Trapping Whelks.

Spearing Wild Moth in the Canaries.

Snaring Eaglets in the Highlands.

Noosing Wild Cats.

Gathering Whiting.

THE GENTLE ART OF CATCHING THINGS

Porpoise Sticking.

HUNTING, SHOOTING AND FISHING

Landing an Anchovy on the Welsh Harp at Hendon.

HUNTING, SHOOTING AND FISHING

"Grousing" in the Valley of the Thames.

HUNTING, SHOOTING AND FISHING

Birdsnesting in the Adirondaks.

HUNTING, SHOOTING AND FISHING

The man who didn't care whether North-going trains went on strike or not.
"If they won't let us leave town in the month of August – well and good."

HUNTING, SHOOTING AND FISHING

A "Sole"-ful Task. Before you go away.
A new exercise for encouraging confidence in fishing from an open boat.

HUNTING, SHOOTING AND FISHING

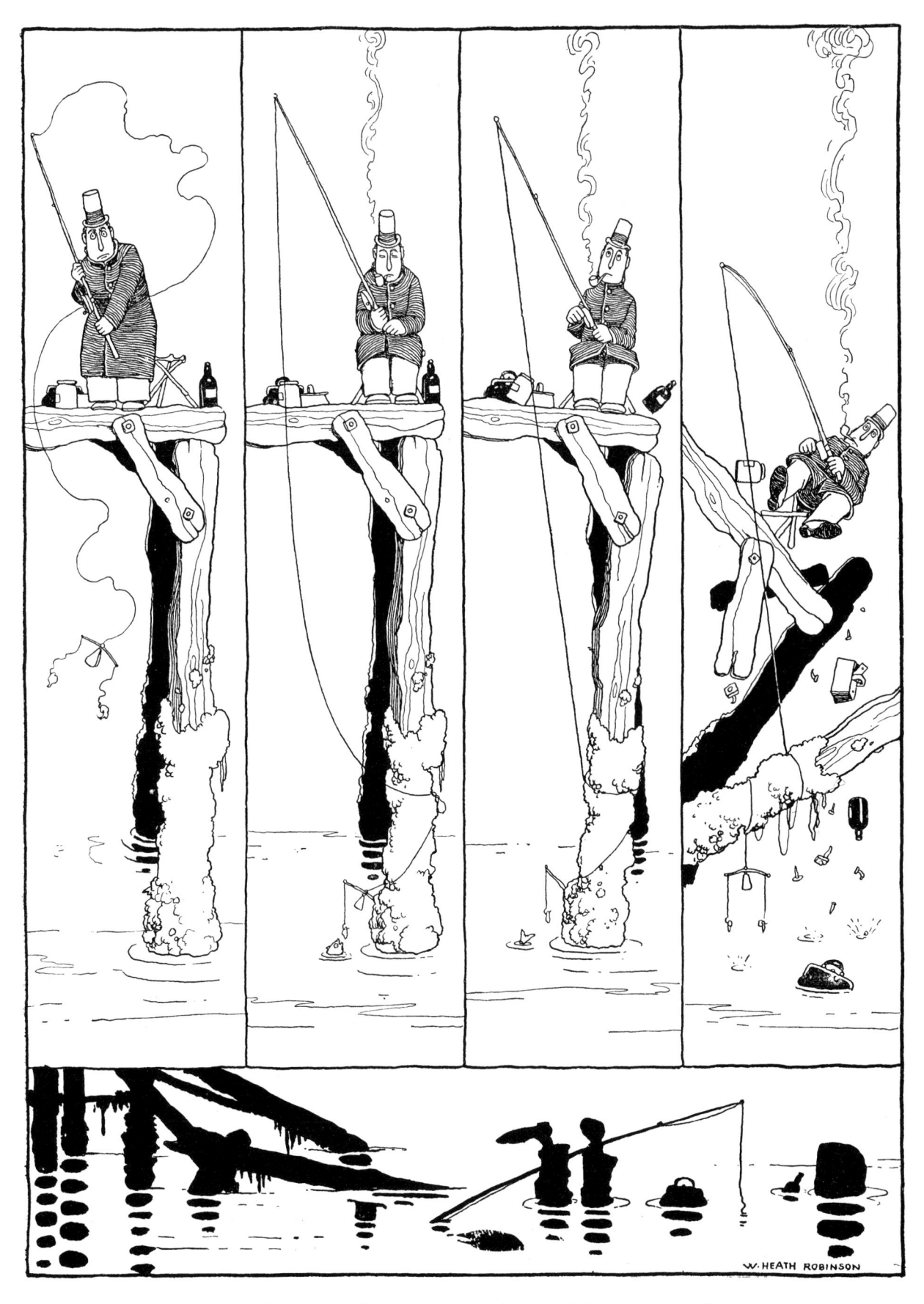

A Moving Picture. Showing a piscatorial tragedy in one short reel.

HUNTING, SHOOTING AND FISHING

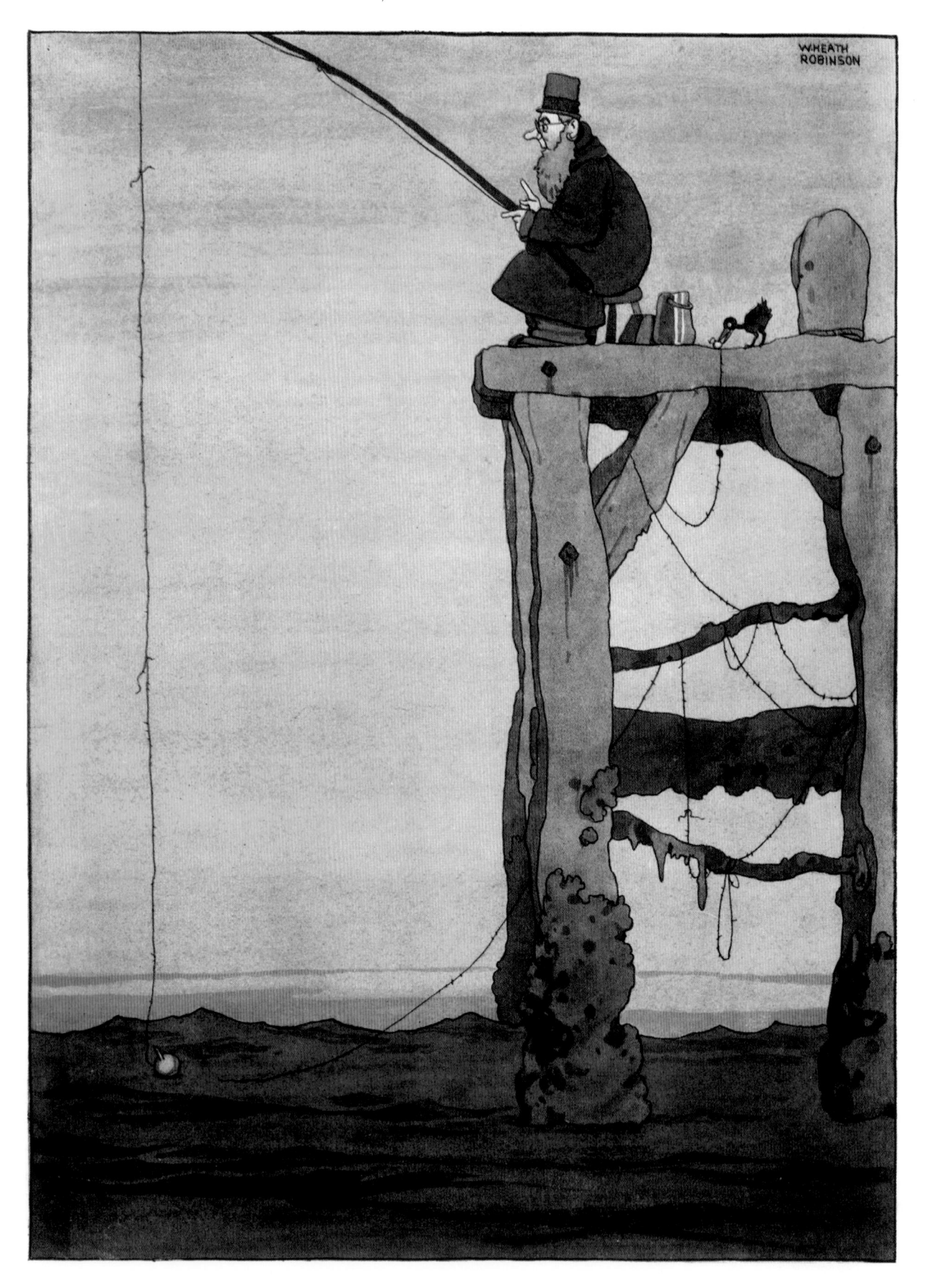

The bite.
A striking example of how patience is sometimes rewarded in angling circles.

The Vicious Circle.
Unsportsmanlike conduct of a trout during the trouting season on Hampstead Ponds.

HUNTING, SHOOTING AND FISHING

How to catch a tiger.

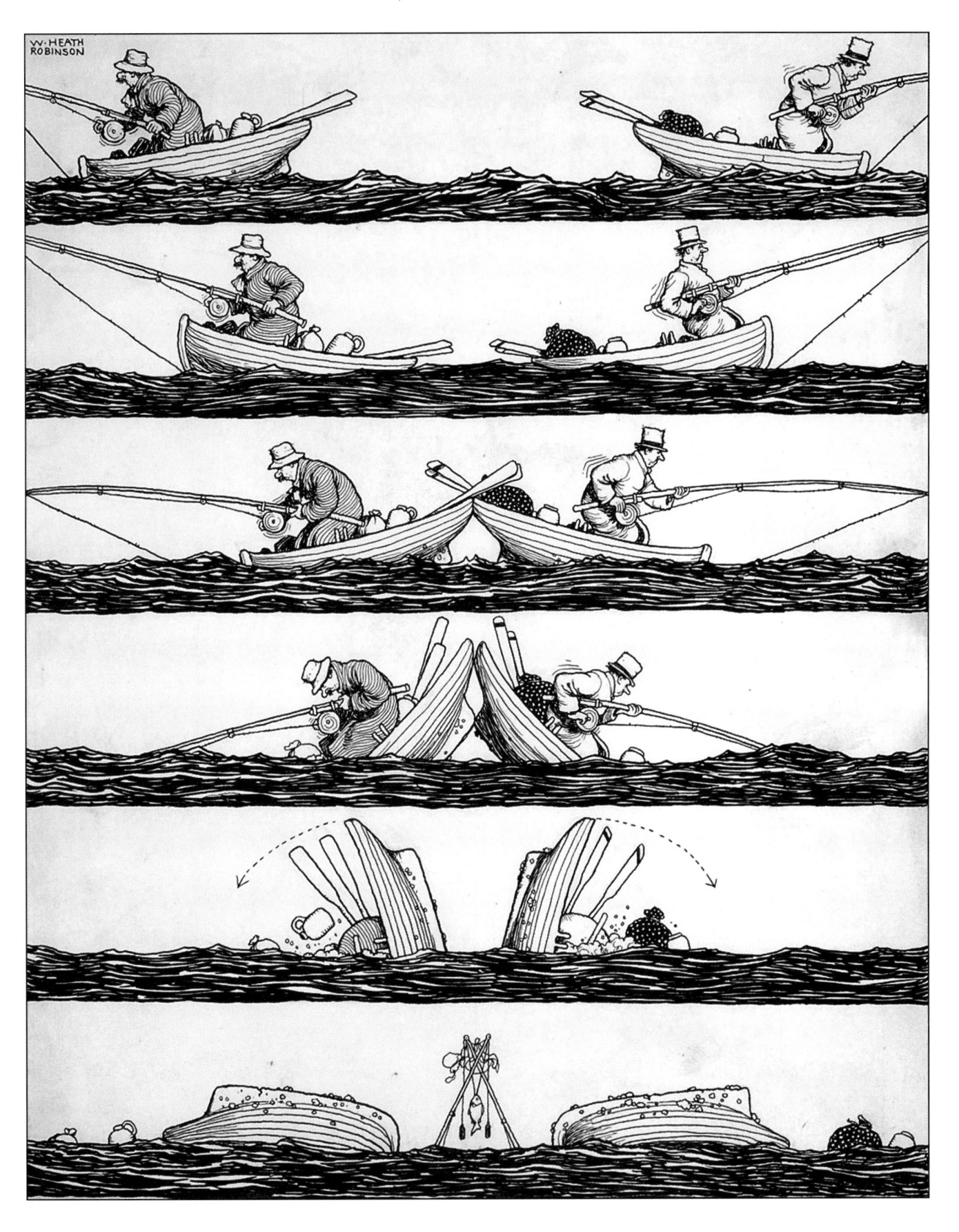

Something on Each Way – A Fish Tragedy.

HUNTING, SHOOTING AND FISHING

Tarpon Fishing de Luxe.

OTHER SPORTS AND GAMES

OTHER SPORTS AND GAMES

A gentle game of rugby in the botanical gardens.

OTHER SPORTS AND GAMES

Cricket: Eton vs Harrow at Lords.

Gathering Edelweiss in the Pyrenees.

OTHER SPORTS AND GAMES

When May is out – Casting Clouts.

For lung power and for the encouragement of elasticity in waiters.

For strength of arm and for power of resistance.

For family transport.

For endurance, and a startling result of over-training.

OTHER SPORTS AND GAMES

The Chukker Chucked. Lost ball!

OTHER SPORTS AND GAMES

Monte-Carlo reformed – Playing snap for filberts.

Sedentary sports – Lawn tennis for the middle aged.

OTHER SPORTS AND GAMES

Safety First - A cricket forecast for 1922.

OTHER SPORTS AND GAMES

GOOD HEAD & TAIL WORK

CLEVER FOOT WORK IN THE SCRUM

More Rugger Trials.
A line-out of Mr (Black) Heath Robinson's Sketch Book which leaves us quite unconverted.

Silly points: how cricket is played in mountainous districts.

"How's That?" Clock Cricket –
a new and exciting summer game for the seaside.

OTHER SPORTS AND GAMES

Putting them on their metal.
The new tennis practice for cultivating a vigorous style.

OTHER SPORTS AND GAMES

Playtime at Wimbledon.
The new craze of jazz tennis caught in full swing by our extra-special artist.

OTHER SPORTS AND GAMES

Another Wash-Out.
How to train at home for your this year's channel swim, affording additional proof that England is a nation of sea-dogs.

"Hey, 'Willow' Waley-O!" Some ingenious suggestions for giving the bowler a better chance. We understand, on Mr. Heath Robinson's authority, that they are to be considered by the MCC as alternatives to the new regulations for smaller cricket balls.

Quick cricket.
A new method of giving both sides a chance of getting in an innings when playing one-day matches.

Cue-ball – a new indoor game combining the subtlety of billiards and the vigour of football.

OTHER SPORTS AND GAMES

Learning to Swim.

OTHER SPORTS AND GAMES

Men will be boys.

ON HOLIDAY

THE NEW HOLIDAY AEROPLANE

ON HOLIDAY

The end of a perfect day.

ON HOLIDAY

The New Aerobathing Machine.
A remarkable invention designed to assist those who "Hesitate upon the brink".

Curious optical illusion caused by a lady forgetting the number of her bathing machine.

"Heath-letics."
Some new water sports for the holidays.

"Heath-letics."
More new water sports for the holidays.

ON HOLIDAY

But if you can't afford a real seaside holiday –
why not try a dust bath in Regent's Park?

Sea Urchins.
The start of the brighter seaside campaign, in anticipation of the holiday season.

ON HOLIDAY

My sweetie went away ... Short sighted gentleman (to his wife):
"Now Jane, you had better cling to my arm; you can never be certain where these quicksands are located."

A Brine Wave.
The birth of the Switch Back and Water Chute idea.

ON HOLIDAY

Soft and "Balmy". The intellectual summer holiday –
as forecast by some of our zealous Seaside Improvements and Morality Associations.

ON HOLIDAY

Foot-sprints on the sands of time. Cautious city man at the end of his holidays getting into form again for his morning sprint against time to catch the morning train.

ON HOLIDAY

Getting fed up! Do we quite realise and appreciate the labours endured by our seaside landladies
to procure us those little delicacies for lunch? Take cod and oyster sauce for example!

ON HOLIDAY

The cleaner bathing movement. Public-spirited endeavours of seaside apartments and boarding-house keepers to remove all impurities and foreign bodies from the water for the convenience of summer bathers.

"The transit of Venus!" An effective ruse of a bashful lady to distract
the attention of onlookers as she runs down to the waves.

ON HOLIDAY

Doing his whack.
A sensible school master devoting three hours of each day during the holidays to keep his hand in.

ON HOLIDAY

"Give" and take. Gentleman who has inadvertently been swallowed up by a quicksand shows great consideration in passing up to his wife her return ticket.

ON HOLIDAY

Sensible measures to be taken in the event of our heatwave continuing.

ON HOLIDAY

Strenuous endeavours to keep the family cool on a warm day at Southend.

ON HOLIDAY

Remarkable presence of mind of cinematographer –
taking an interesting close-up of himself as he accidentally falls from the top of Beachy Head.

ON HOLIDAY

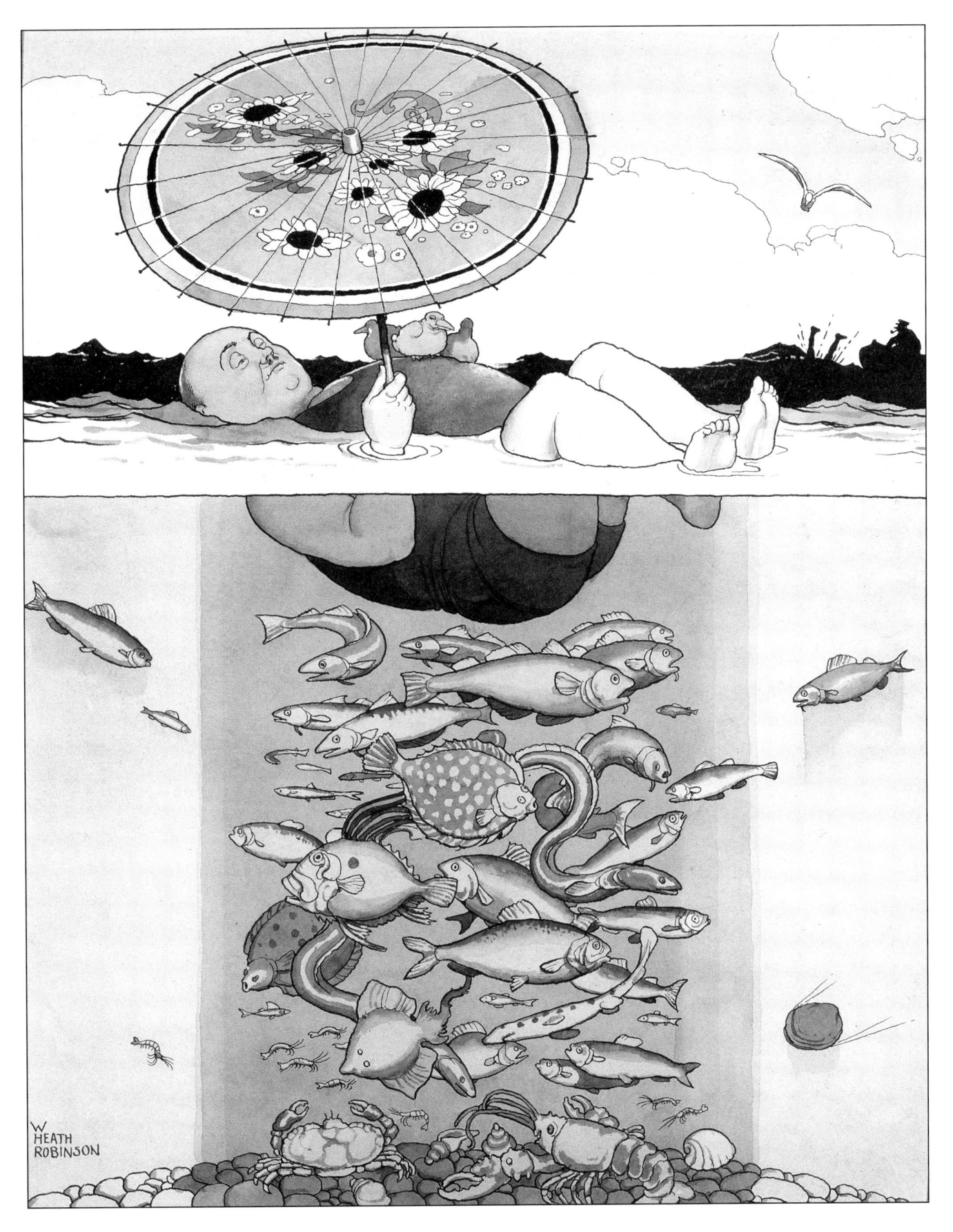

Grateful Shade.

ON HOLIDAY

Cover for Humorist Summer Number 1936.

ON HOLIDAY

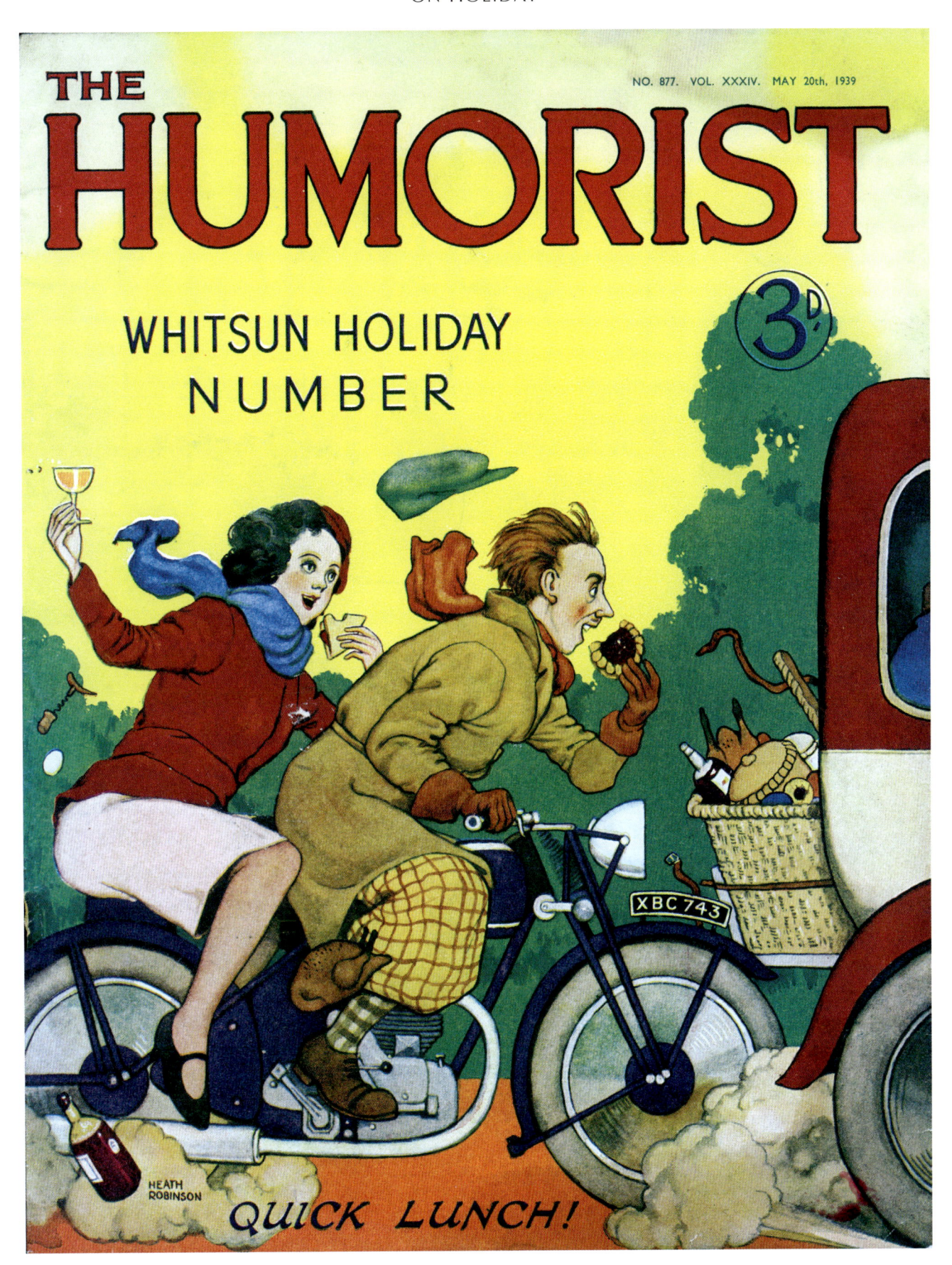

"Quick Lunch" –
Cover for Humorist Whitsun Holiday special number 1939.

ON HOLIDAY

The Disturbed Nap.

ON HOLIDAY

Free Seats.

ON HOLIDAY

New Seaside Sports.

MOTORING

The last straw.

CARTASTROPHIES

Bogged.

Uncowed.

The broken pipe.

The too-sudden turn.

Subsidence on the Brighton Road.

MOTORING

Elasticity.

MOTORING

The Water Coupe.

MOTORING

A heavy snowstorm –

120

MOTORING

– and a rapid thaw.

An Awkward Predicament.

COURTING

COURTING

The Reprimand.

COURTING

How the trains get delayed on the London, Brighton and South Coast Railway.
Nothing of this sort happened when the volunteers ran the trains during the strike.

The "Write" of way. Love at first sight.

COURTING

The fall of the year. The sort of unfortunate happening that must inevitably spoil the efforts of even the best super-film producers in autumnal settings.

COURTING

Wherefore art thou radio? It has been suggested that during the Spring, 2LO should devote one night a week to amatory music for those under the subtle influence of the vernal season.

COURTING

The maid and the magician.
A real-life film in three terrible reels!

COURTING

"Oh, will thou be my Valentine". A graceful tableau staged by a well-known member of the Stock Exchange as a pleasant surprise for the wife of his bosom on St. Valentine's morn.

"'Tis an ill wind that ..."

COURTING

Hoisting the Chaperone.

COURTING

The Language of Eggs. Some new designs for Easter eggs to facilitate the
exchange of graceful sentiments and amorous messages.

COURTING

Opportunity.

COURTING

A near thing.

COURTING

A Terrible Blow!
The sad story of a punctured romance told in four moving chapters.

AT HOME

AT HOME

Mother's help.

SPRING CLEANING IN FULL SWING

Breakfast.

SPRING CLEANING IN FULL SWING

The disorder of the bath.

SPRING CLEANING IN FULL SWING

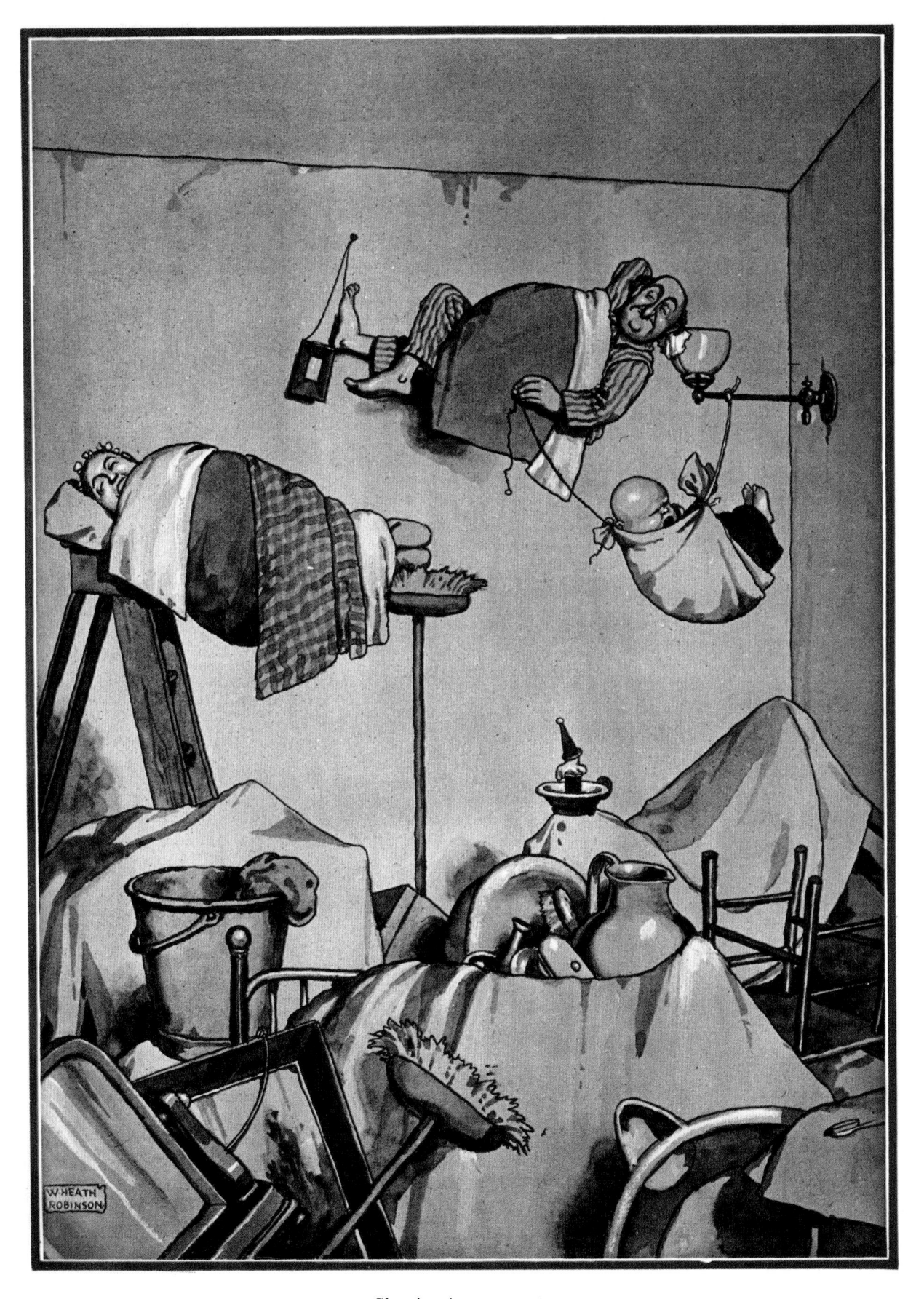

Sleeping Arrangements.

SPRING CLEANING IN FULL SWING

Getting out of the house.

SPRING CLEANING IN FULL SWING

Coming down to breakfast.

SPRING CLEANING IN FULL SWING

His only shaving glass.

AT HOME

Leading from dummy.
One of our most popular hostesses conducting a full-dress rehearsal of her first at-home of the season.

AT HOME

Reforming the Dance. The Congregational Union has recently given a qualified approval to dancing. If Mr. Robinson's suggestion were carried out, we feel sure that the dance would meet with the support of even the most puritanically minded.

AT HOME

Mrs Snifkin, dreamily, as she smells burning –
"Dear! Dear! He's smoking that cheap tobacco again."

Weighty Matters –
An unrecorded eclipse of the sun.

Pets' corners, Boldersbury Mansions, SW.

AT HOME

The extending bungalow for weekend parties.

RADIO

My delicate aerial – modern style. A tragedy of Christmas Eve.

RADIO

Listening in –
that aerial vibration.

A wireless (up)set. WIRELESS ENTHUSIAST (to sympathetic neighbour):
"Yes, it is quite alright in theory, but somehow or other in practice the wretched thing won't work,"

RADIO

A stormy night at the listening inn.
A hitherto unrecorded incidence of a building being saved by wireless during an equinoctial gale.

The timely call of a new world.
A wireless fan during one of recent earth tremors in the Midlands just receiving America.

RADIO

Up the Bole.
Curious disguise assumed by wireless enthusiast to escape payment of his licence.

A Bedtime Story. The broadcaster (after a heavy day of it): London Calling. It is now six minutes past eleven and we will all go over to the Savoy Hotel for dance music (aside) I don't think!

RADIO

The Broadcast Play.
How they make the sound effects.

Some new wireless tests.

THE BRITISH CHARACTER

A FEW VIRTUES

Chivalry.

A FEW VIRTUES

Devotion.

A FEW VIRTUES

Charity.

A FEW VIRTUES

Self-Sacrifice.

A JAMBOREE OF LAUGHTER

Resting the forelegs of a tired camel.

Catching a lady passenger who has fallen from an airship.

A JAMBOREE OF LAUGHTER

Laudable attempt to cure a Giraffe's sore throat, made by a kind-hearted Scout.

A JAMBOREE OF LAUGHTER

Shipwrecked Scout saving the situation by courageous signalling act.

A JAMBOREE OF LAUGHTER

Generous young Scout exchanging clothes with a ragged stranger.

A JAMBOREE OF LAUGHTER

Priceless young Scout provides a half-holiday for an organ grinder's monkey.

THE BRITISH CHARACTER

Croc(k)ed! –
Pictorial proof of the famous adage that "An Englishman never knows when he is eaten".

THE RIGHT SPIRIT

A quiet game of snap is a great aid to maintaining
the right spirit when snowed-up ....

THE RIGHT SPIRIT

A cordial greeting.
Mr William Sikes saves the situation.

THE RIGHT SPIRIT

The gentle game of snowballing as it should be played ...

THE RIGHT SPIRIT

The right and seasonable way of behaving in an unexpected encounter.

THE RIGHT SPIRIT

Mistletoe and a little game of "Oranges and Lemons"
would bring the Christmas spirit ...

THE RIGHT SPIRIT

There is always a bright side to the many little mishaps –

THE RIGHT SPIRIT

– that may spoil our Christmas if we fail to regard them in the right light.

THE RIGHT SPIRIT

Keep smiling even if the ice cracks.
Don't let little worries upset your Christmas.

GARDENING

MORE HINTS TO AMATEUR GARDENERS

New methods of lightening a heavy soil.

MORE HINTS TO AMATEUR GARDENERS

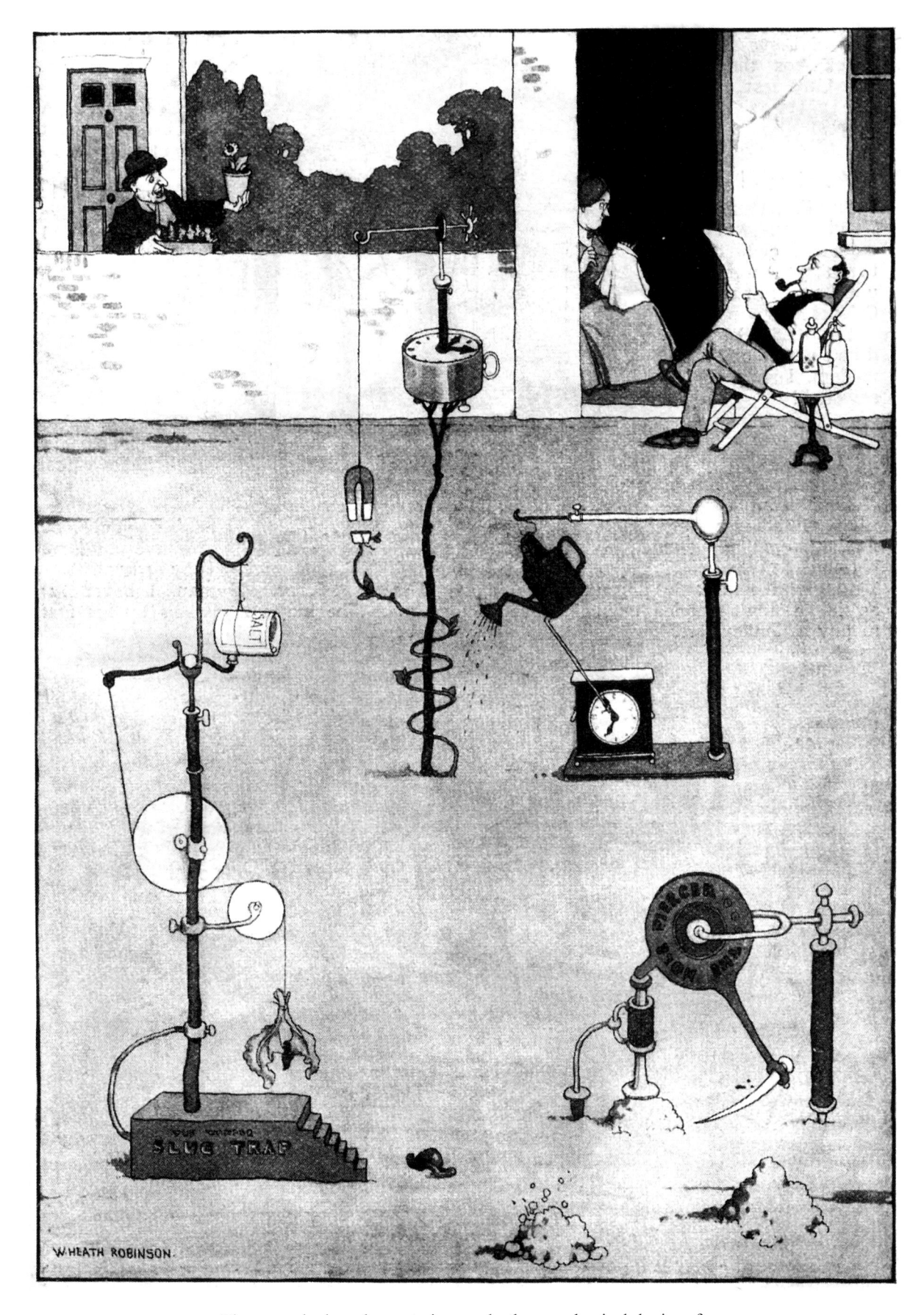

The new clockwork pea trainer and other mechanical devices for
lightening the labour of the amateur.

MORE HINTS TO AMATEUR GARDENERS

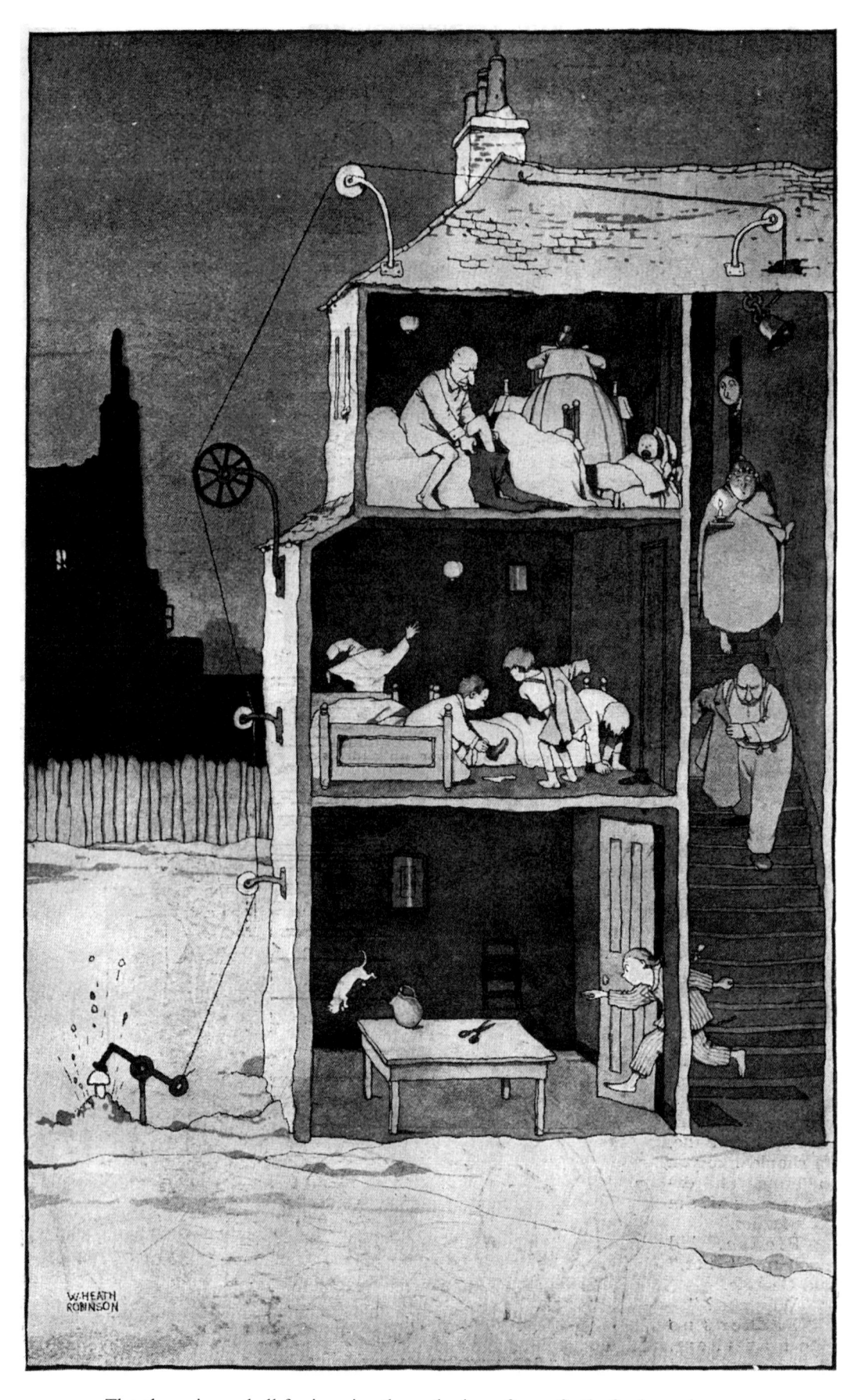

The champignon bell for insuring the gathering of a perfectly fresh mushroom

GARDENING

The new fruit tree pruner with ingenious adjustment for automatically lime-washing the bark while pruning the branches.

GARDENING

Hints for the Amateur Landscape Gardener.

A Highly Complicated Science

By K. R. G. BROWNE

With Pictures by W. HEATH ROBINSON

IT was Napoleon, I believe, who once remarked laughingly to Josephine across the teacups: "These English are a nation of gardeners! *Zut, alors!*"

A pretty shrewd remark, in my opinion. Of every ten Englishmen accosted at random in the street—somewhat to their surprise, no doubt—probably at least six would prove to be keen amateurs of the trowel, the shears, and the twopenny seed-packet. The other four would start nervously and hurry on, suspecting a catch somewhere.

In their earliest form, presumably, gardens were merely bits of ground on which things either grew or did not. It is likely, indeed, that the early British caveholder never even realized that he had a garden until flowers actually sprouted on his premises. Nowadays, however, gardening is a highly complicated science, bristling with Latin phrases and giving enjoyment to a large number of people; and it is for the benefit of the less experienced of the latter that the following elementary hints have been compiled and fitted with tasteful illustrations.

Obviously, the chief problem confronting the gardener is that of deciding what to plant, and where, and even why. According to the experts, his first step should be to select a few trees and shrubs, as these will temper the wind to the shorn violet in inclement weather, while on summer afternoons their shade is very pleasant to recline in with a good book. Washing can also be hung out on them, if it is that kind of neighbourhood.

In selecting his shrubs, the beginner need not be deterred by their extensive Latin names, as these are only added to make it more difficult and usually mean something quite simple, such as a gum-tree. *Polygala chamæbuxus*, for example (which is often mistaken by novices for a

By installing loud-speakers at strategic points the gardener can roar abuse at intrusive wildfowl without interrupting his meals.

A Highly Complicated Science

To safeguard windfalls against bruising.

Caucasian potentate or a disease of the inner ear), is only six inches high and can be carried in one hand; while *ulex* is not, as some people suppose, a patent remedy for digestive disorders, but simply a gorse-bush.

In the matter of flowers, of course, the gardener must obey the dictates of his heart. Some hold that roses are the only possible flora for horticulturists of taste; and, indeed, there is something very attractive about such specimens as Lady Bilch-Overspoon (glossy pink: very large), Fifi Mechante (creamy pink: very free and beautiful), and General Quacklingham (rich velvety crimson: very strong). Others pin their faith to tulips, dahlias and the like, while yet others prefer the simpler hardy annuals—such as phlox, larkspur, love-in-a-mist, fun-in-a-belfry, coreopsis, ellipsis, mignonette, bishop's nightshirt and eschscholtzia (which is generally spelt "Californian poppy," to the relief of all)—that can be trusted to do their stuff with the minimum of supervision.

The gardener, however, must not suppose that his labours are completed when he has chosen and planted all his flora and/or veg., and that he can just sit back and wait for things to grow. For Nature, in her inscrutable wisdom, has decreed that where there is a garden there shall also be (*a*) plenty of weeds and (*b*) considerable insect-life, red in tooth and claw and eager to gnaw holes in and ruin anything from a pansy to a hollyhock.

Weeds, if left to riot unchecked, can overrun a garden in less time than it takes to say "*Xerophyllum Asphodeloides*, the famous Athenian philosopher." Merely to wrench the top off a weed, leaving its roots to fester underground, is to ensure that the beastly thing will bloom again at its earliest convenience: the entire growth must be

With a little forethought trees can be pruned to accommodate a clothes-line.

scooped out of the soil and flung over the fence.

Where weeding is concerned, people who stoop slowly and with reluctance naturally will not get such quick results as those who bend featly and without discomfort; and, obviously, they will require stouter braces. I would recommend all such, therefore, to employ the Heath Robinson "Peter Pan" Eeziweeda, here illustrated. This is a kind of small travelling-crane of one-woman-power, which enables the weedsman to take the weight off his feet and quarter the garden thoroughly without either succumbing to apoplexy or treading on the tulips. A simpler but somewhat similar device, consisting chiefly of a strong belt and a small hand-operated winch, is also shown for the benefit of indifferent stoopers who prefer to be independent of the little woman.

As insects, unlike weeds, are loth to stand still and let the gardener rebuke them, it is often necessary to employ guile when coping with the earwigs, wireworms, greenfly, weevils, cockchafers and other aphides which, if allowed to multiply and have fun, can make the toughest garden look deplorably second-hand.

Most of these little pests are oddly susceptible to the scent of tobacco, and will fall into a swoon on being briskly smoked at or sprayed with powdered snuff. Once unconscious, they can be packed in bundles of ten

The Eeziweeda, for weeding the garden without treading on the beds.

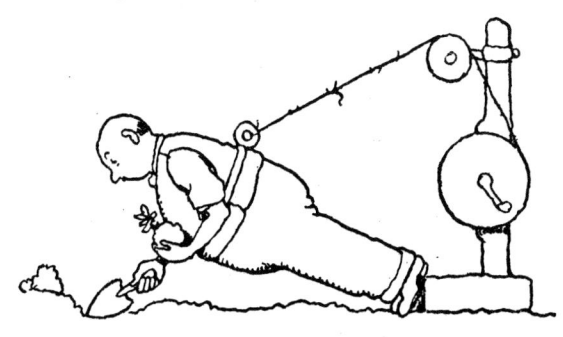

Device for the prevention of gardener's backache.

and forwarded to the Chancellor of the Exchequer in the guise of "conscience-money." When employing the snuff-gambit, the gardener —to avoid spraying the people next door, and thereby giving rise to ill-feeling and possibly the exchange of invective—is advised to use the curvilinear re-entrant type of snuff-spray, as illustrated, thus ensuring that any resultant sneezing will occur on his side of the fence.

Thoughtless birds, again, can do a lot of damage to a garden. Our feathered friends— and notably the sparrow, the starling, the common vulture and the greater whey-faced piefinch, or Peabody's Puffin—have no respect

A Highly Complicated Science

for innocent young flowers and regard a newly-sown lawn as a kind of quick-lunch counter. A fine-meshed net, completely covering the garden, will usually baffle these marauders; but many gardeners, contending that this lets in the rain and interferes with the tennis, prefer to discourage them with buckshot.

A more humane method, perhaps, is to engage a qualified bird-scarer, or dance-band vocalist, who has been trained to twirl a police-rattle and cry "Shoo! Shoo!" at intervals. If this is impracticable for economic reasons, one can get the same result by installing half a dozen loud-speakers at strategic points about the premises and messuage, and connecting them to a microphone in the dining-room. By this means the gardener can roar abuse at intrusive pelicans and other wildfowl without interrupting his meals.

It is quite wrong, by the way, to suppose that a garden needs attention only in the summer, and that for the rest of the year the gardener can devote his leisure exclusively to amateur conjuring or the breeding of pedigree newts. If it is to give of its best, a garden must be cherished all the year round. The conscientious gardener must be continually on the job, toiling, rejoicing, and borrowing the essential implements from kindly neighbours.

During the autumn and winter various measures must be taken to protect plants of frail physique from cold spells, thunderstorms and similar climatic hazards. These measures include the provision of inexpensive umbrellas to

A greenhouse for the flower-loving flat-dweller.

A well-trained tree.

shield young blooms from tempests, the attachment of a lightning-conductor to the gardener's own hat, and the swaddling of valuable bushes against chill zephyrs from the east.

The saddening influence of falling leaves upon the sensitive observer has often been described by poets who have run out of Spring material; but falling apples, torn from their moorings by autumnal gusts, are equally depressing to the thrifty gardener who had been relying on them to help him out with his greengrocer's bill, as fruit that has bounced even once loses much of its value as pie-matter. To protect such windfalls, however, from abrasions, it is only necessary to surround the base of the tree with a few mattresses, divers cushions, and any sponges that are not in use at the moment.

There are certain plants—e.g., tomatoes and orchids—which are so susceptible to weather conditions that they can only be reared successfully under glass in a more or less African temperature. Gardeners of mature years and a portly habit are apt to find this atmosphere exhausting, and to emerge from a visit to the greenhouse in a gravely overheated condition and a hopelessly wilted collar. The most sensible costume, therefore, for ministering to tomatoes is a common or (in this case) garden bathing-suit, let the neighbours whisper as they may. Gardeners who, having no greenhouse, are suddenly called upon to warm up an ailing aspidistra can do the job with the help of a hot-water-bottle, a thermometer, and the simple apparatus here depicted.

But what, it may be asked, about the flower-loving flat-dweller? Lacking not only a greenhouse, but a garden in which to put it, must he be denied the joy of watching two orchids grow where but one plantain grew before?

The curvilinear re-entrant snuff-spray prevents spraying the people next door.

Warming up the aspidistra.

By no means. As the illustration shows, it is a simple matter to affix a greenhouse to any convenient window. (It should be affixed carefully, however, and used only with discretion, as passers-by who have been stunned by falling flower-pots are liable to take considerable umbrage and possibly legal action.) Warmed by uncostly oil-stoves and adding a touch of colour to the otherwise sombre street, these embellishments increase the value of the property and enable the tenant to enjoy all the delights of horticulture at no risk of getting his feet wet. In cold weather, too, small delicate children can be parked in them for short periods, with great benefit to their little constitutions.

In conclusion, perhaps, it should be added that no reference is intended to any living vegetable, and that practically everything mentioned (except Mr. Heath Robinson and a few other things) is almost laughably fictitious.

ACKNOWLEDGEMENTS

We are grateful to the following organisations that have provided images for this book.

Chris Beetles Limited.
Pages 21, 22, 23, 24, 25, 26, 31, 32, 52, 59, 62, 63, 69, 71, 75, 78, 82, 83, 102, 103, 104, 105, 110, 120. 121, 129, 131, 133, 147, 148, 149, 150, 159, 185.

Mary Evans Picture Library.
Pages 2, 6, 16, 17, 18, 19, 20, 27, 28, 29, 30, 34, 35, 36, 39, 40, 41, 42, 50, 51, 53, 54, 55, 56, 57, 70, 72, 73, 74, 76, 77, 78, 79, 81, 86, 87, 88, 89, 90, 92, 93, 94, 96, 97, 98, 99, 100, 101, 107, 125, 126, 127, 128, 130, 136, 139, 140, 141, 142, 143, 144, 145, 146, 152, 153, 154, 155, 156, 157, 158, 172.

The William Heath Robinson Trust.
Page 95.

Other images from a private collection.